for 1000+ tutorials ... use our
free site .... drawinghowtodraw.com

BY RACHEL A GOLDSTEIN

DRAWING FOR JEWISH KIDS

WITH HEBREW LETTERS IN EASY STEPS

CARTOONING AND LEARNING HOW TO DRAW KAWAII CARTOONS WITH HEBREW LETTERS

ALEPH PENCIL BOY AND ICE CREAM

1.

2.

3.

Letter 'M'

4.

5.

Erase on Dotted Line.

6.

↓ NOW YOU TRY ↓

BET HAPPY ROBOT

1.

2.

3.

4.

5.

6.

⬇ NOW YOU TRY ⬇

GIMMEL SITTING BIRD

1.

2.

3.

4.

5.

#3 Shapes →

6.

Letter 'U'
Shapes
↓

↓ NOW YOU TRY ↓

DALET CUTE CRITTERS

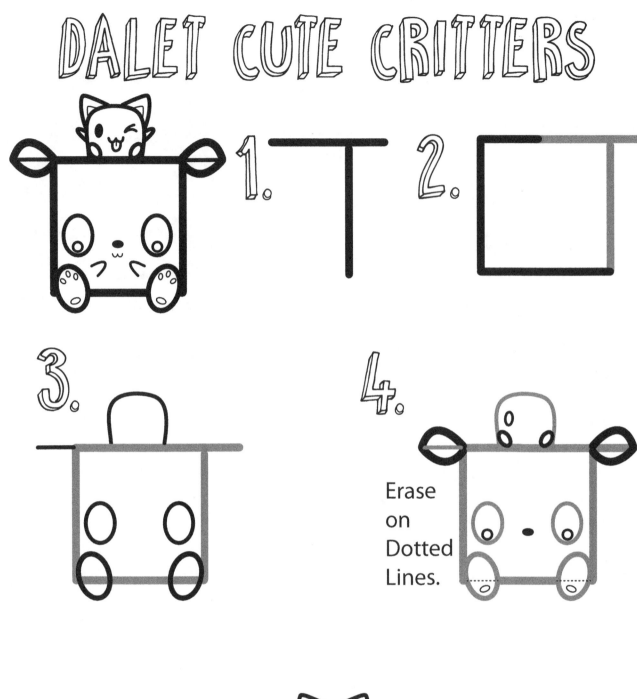

1.

2.

3.

4. Erase on Dotted Lines.

5. #3 Shapes

6.

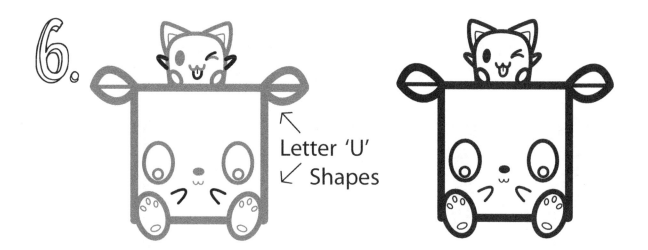

Letter 'U'
Shapes

↓ NOW YOU TRY ↓

HEY STANDING BOY

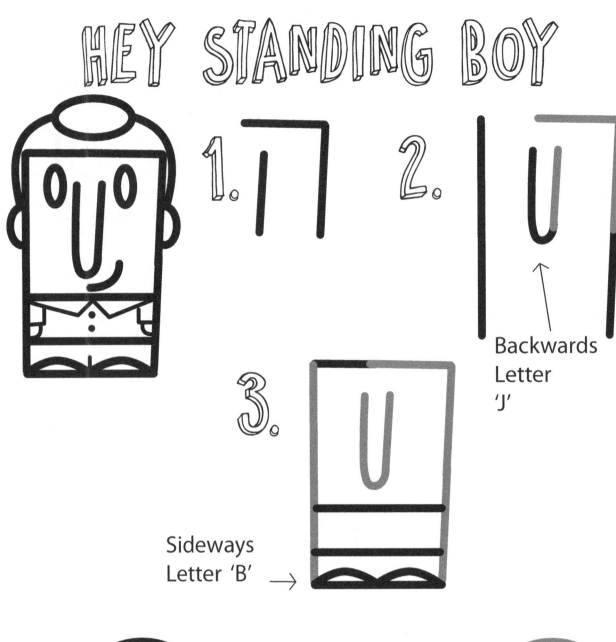

1.

2.

Backwards Letter 'J'

3.

Sideways Letter 'B' →

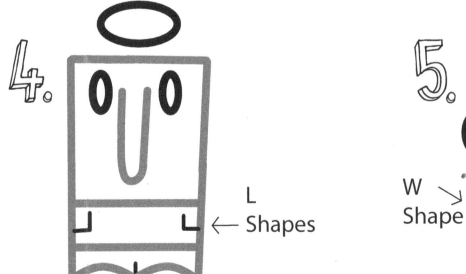

4.

L Shapes →

5.

W Shape

6.

Don't draw the dotted line.

↓ NOW YOU TRY ↓

7.

#3 Shaped
← Hand

↓ NOW YOU TRY ↓

ZAYIN CUTIE PIE BUNNY

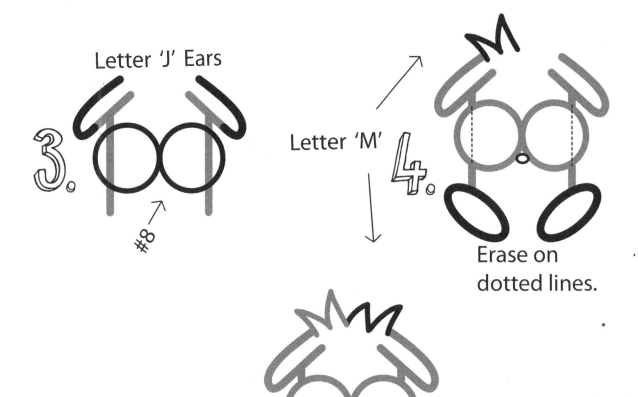

1.

2.

3. Letter 'J' Ears

#8

4. Letter 'M'

Erase on dotted lines.

5.

6.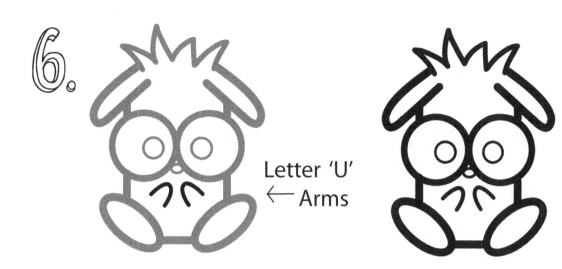

Letter 'U'
← Arms

↓ NOW YOU TRY ↓

CHET LOVING COUPLE

1.

2.

3.

'm'
shape

#9
Shapes

4.

B   B   ← #3 +
                  'U'
                → Shapes

Erase on dotted lines.

5.

#9
Shapes

6.

'?' Shape

↓ NOW YOU TRY ↓

TET CUTE KITTY

1.

2.
Don't draw the dotted line.

3.
↑
#3 Shape

4.
← Sideways '?' Shape

5.

↓ NOW YOU TRY ↓

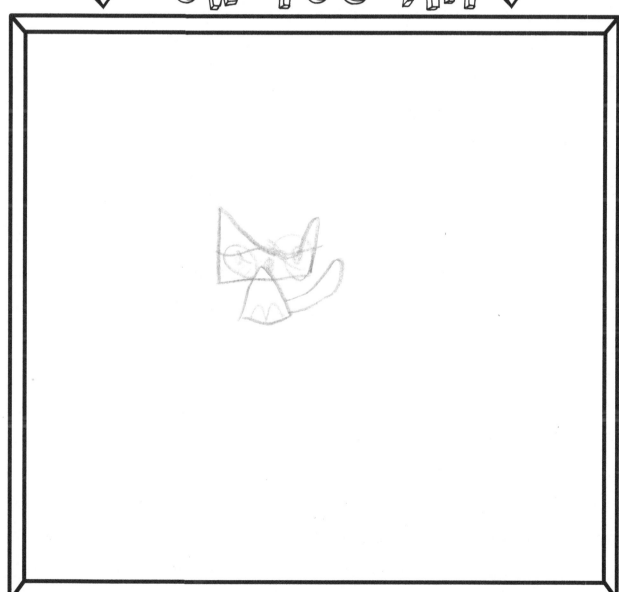

YOD CURIOUS BIRDY

1. ⌐

2.  #8 Shape

Don't draw ↑
the dotted line.

3.

4.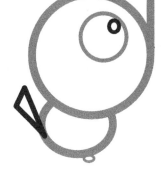

Sideways Letter 'V'

5.

6.

Letter 'C'
Shape

↓ NOW YOU TRY ↓

KAF BABY DINO

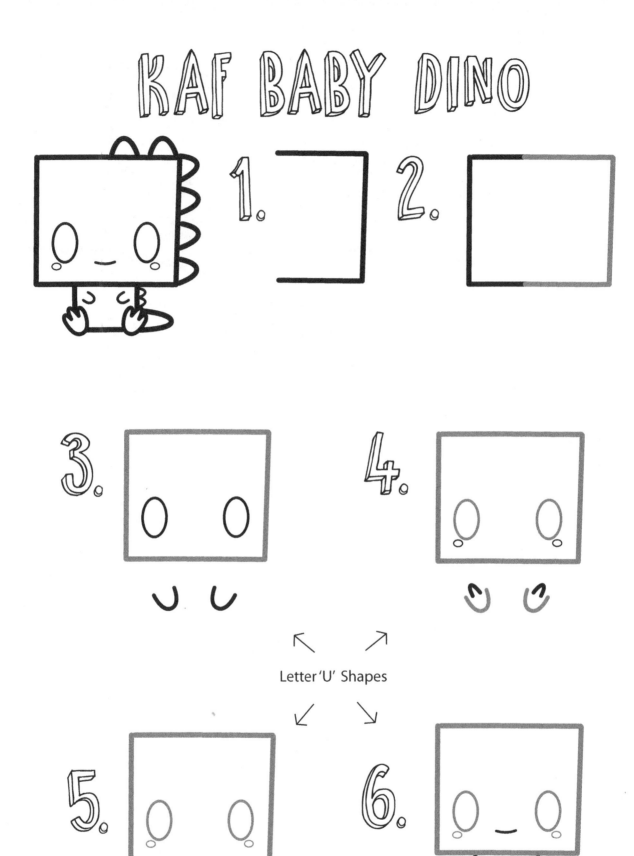

1.

2.

3.

4.

Letter 'U' Shapes

5.

6.

7.

↓ NOW YOU TRY ↓

FINAL KAF LOVE BUNNY

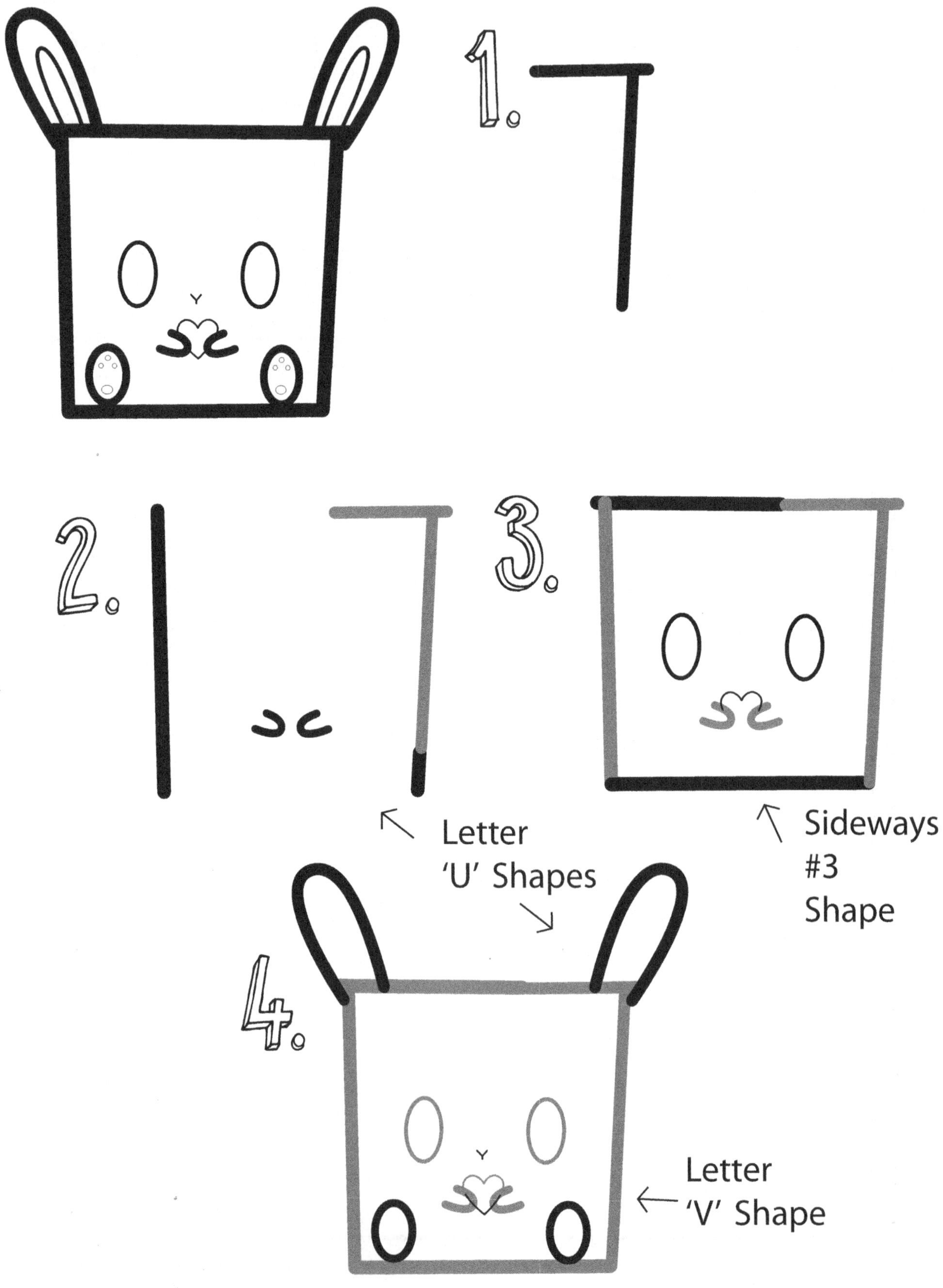

1.

2.

← Letter 'U' Shapes

3.

↑ Sideways #3 Shape

4.

Letter 'V' Shape ←

5.

↓ NOW YOU TRY ↓

LAMED LAUGHY GUY

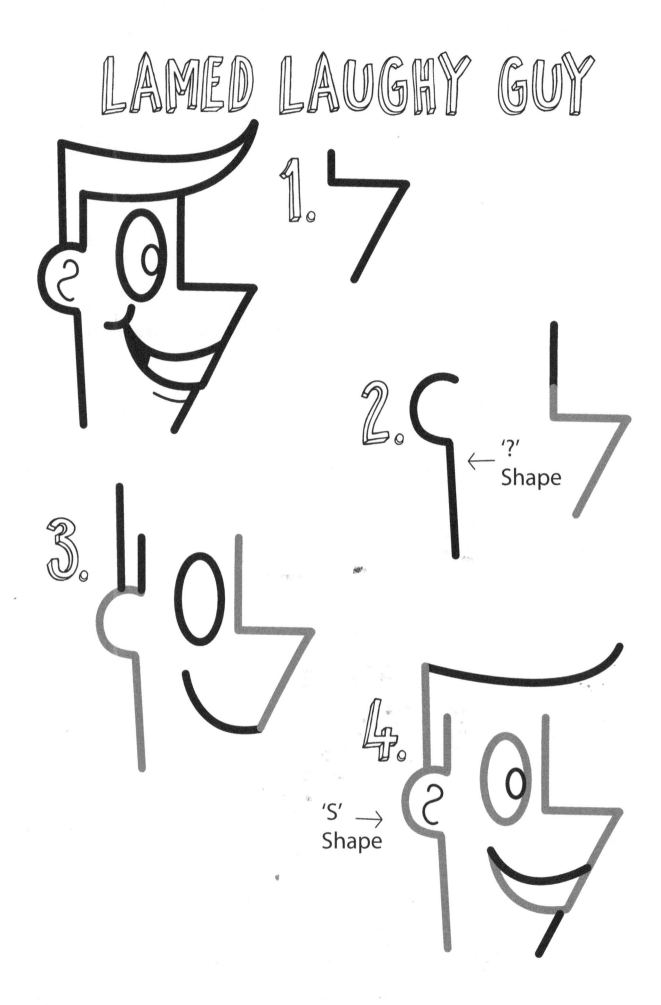

1.

2. ← '?' Shape

3.

4. 'S' → Shape

5.

↓ NOW YOU TRY ↓

MEM UNICORN

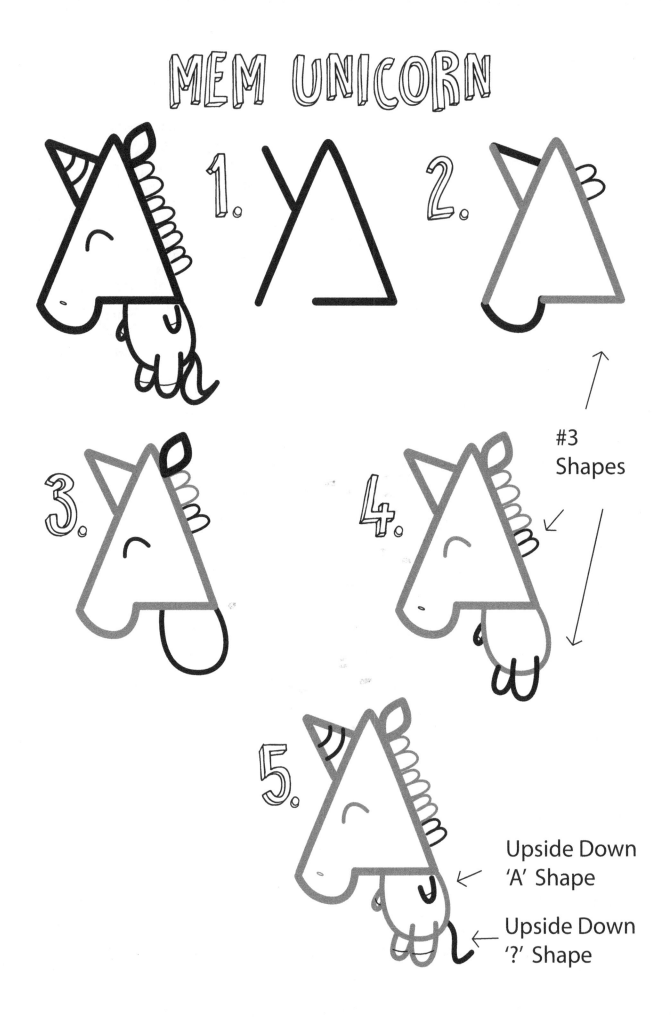

1.

2.

#3 Shapes

3.

4.

5.

Upside Down 'A' Shape

Upside Down '?' Shape

6.

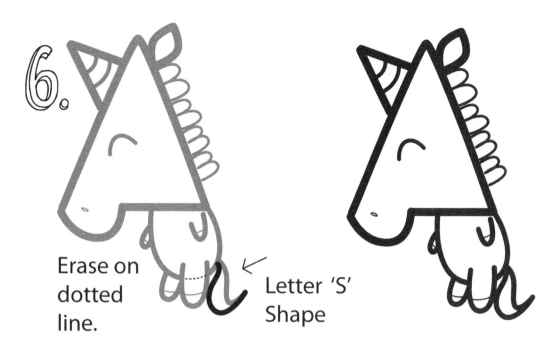

Erase on
dotted
line.

Letter 'S'
Shape

↓ NOW YOU TRY ↓

FINAL MEM LOVE WHALE

1.

2.

#8

3.

Erase on dotted lines.

#3 Shapes

Letter 'V' Shapes

4.

5.

Sideways
Letter
'F'
Shape

↓ NOW YOU TRY ↓

NUN CUTIE PIE BABY

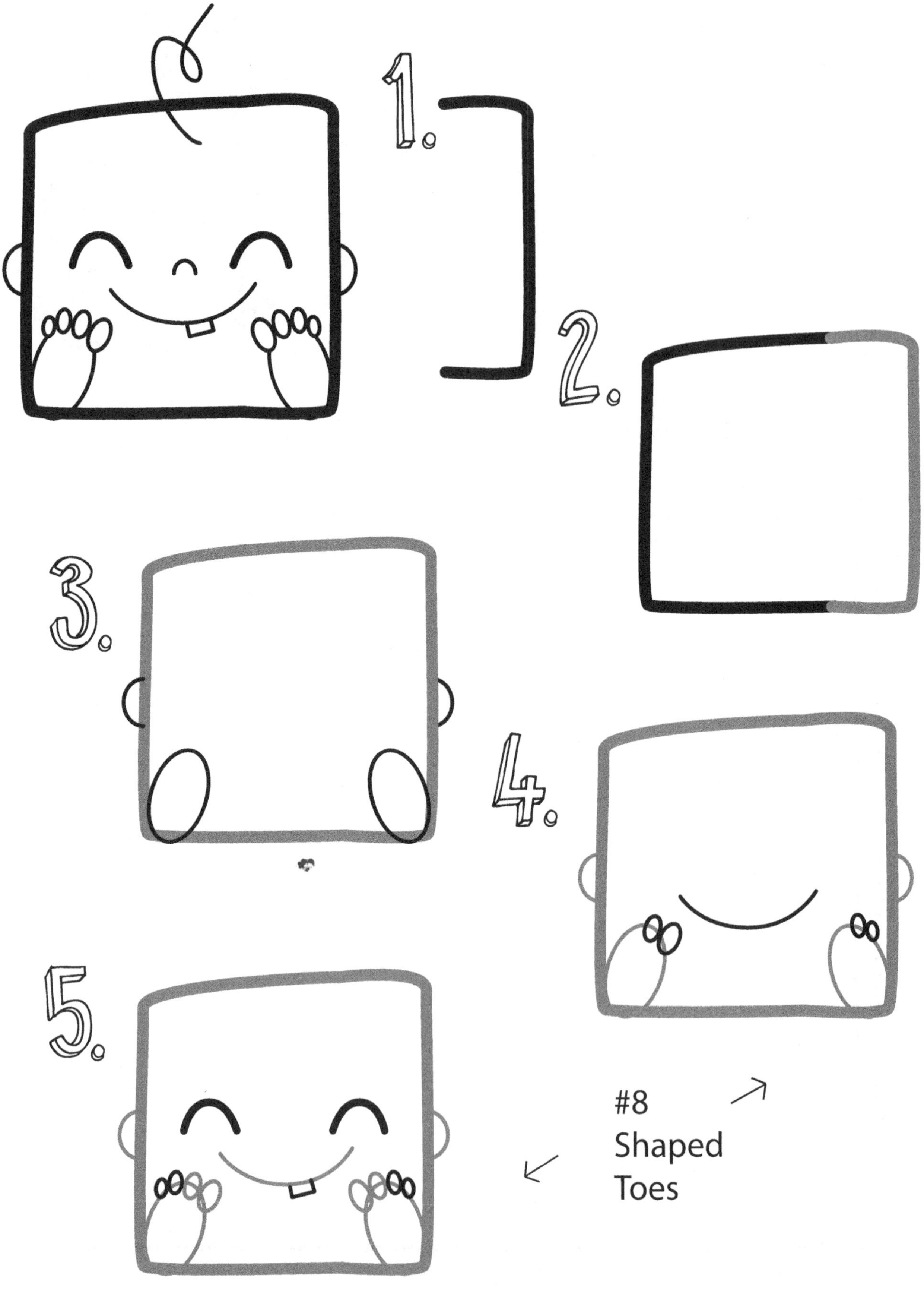

1.

2.

3.

4.

5.

#8
Shaped
Toes

6.

Erase on dotted lines.

↓ NOW YOU TRY ↓

FINAL NUN BABY GIRAFFE

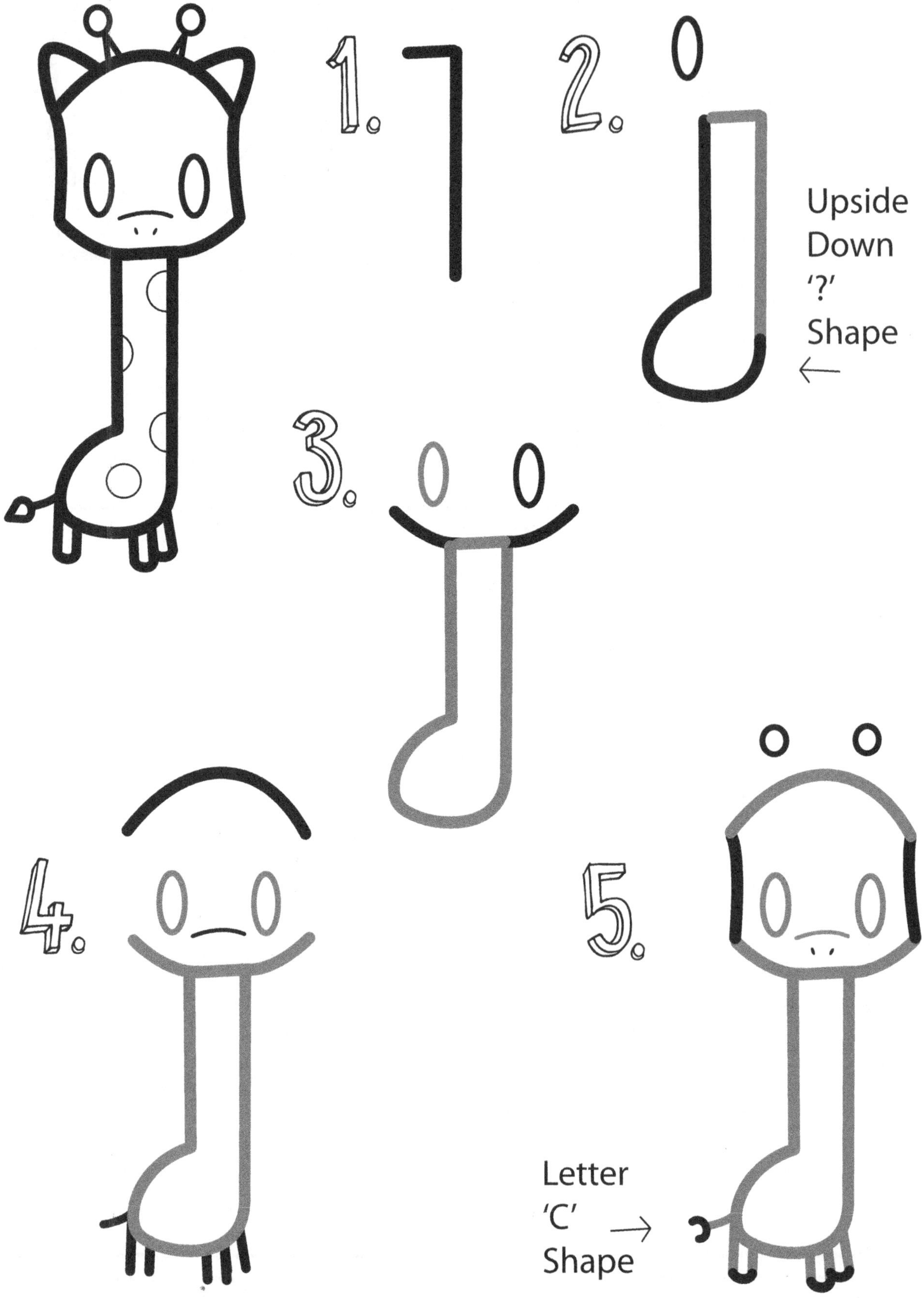

1.

2.

Upside
Down
'?'
Shape

3.

4.

5.

Letter
'C'
Shape

6.

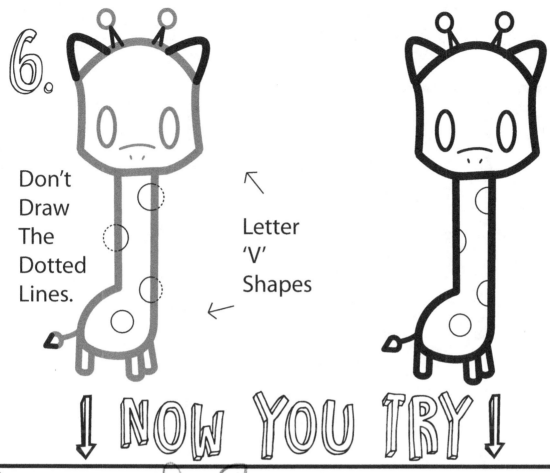

Don't Draw The Dotted Lines.

Letter 'V' Shapes

↓ NOW YOU TRY ↓

SAMECH BABY ELEPHANT

1.

2.

3.

4.

5.

6. Erase on dotted line.

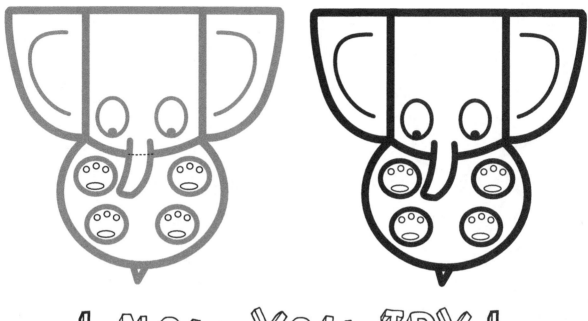

AYIN GIRL AND KITTEN

1.

2.

Upside Down '?' Shape →

3.

Letters 'A' + ← 't' ←

4. 'C' + 'A' Shapes

5. Letter 'W'

6.

↓ NOW YOU TRY ↓

PEY CUTE DRAGON

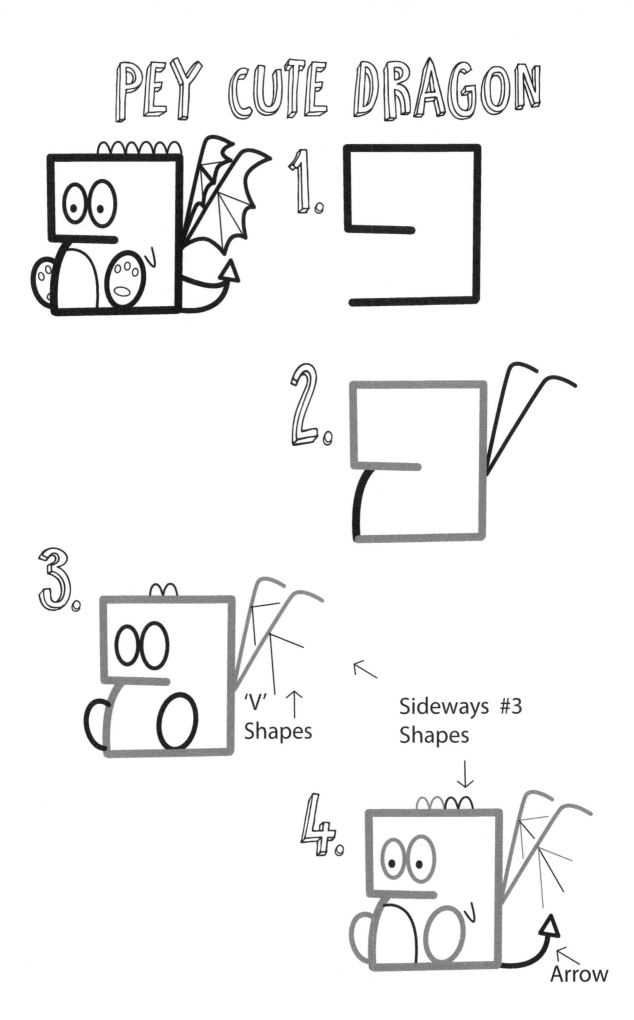

1.

2.

3.

'V' Shapes

Sideways #3 Shapes

4.

Arrow

5.

Draw Curved Lines Between
Each of the Lines on the Wings

FINAL PEY SITTING COW

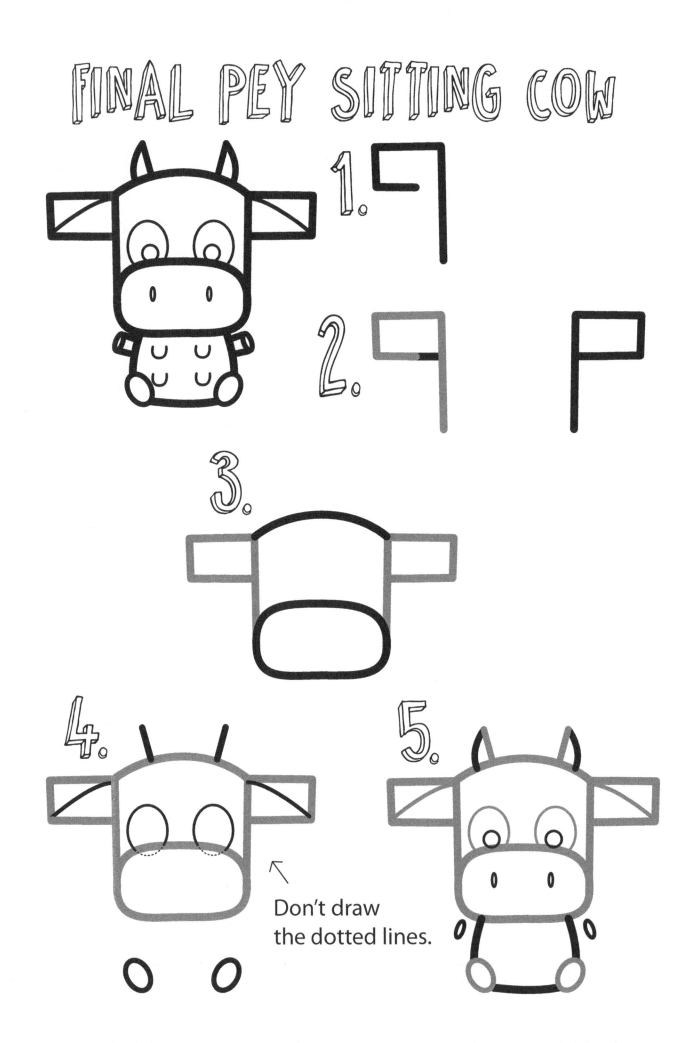

Don't draw
the dotted lines.

6.

↓ NOW YOU TRY ↓

TSADE OPOSSUM FAMILY

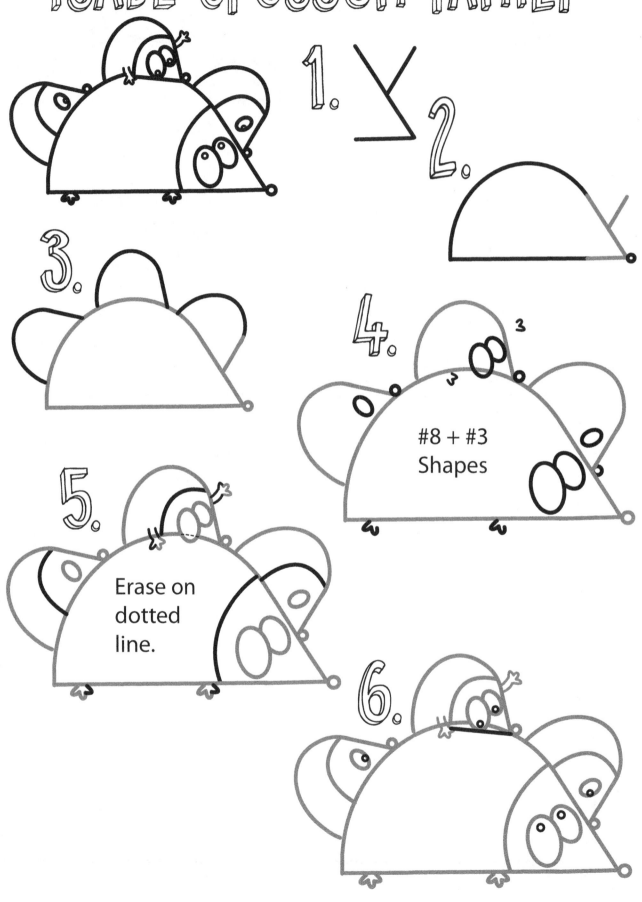

1.

2.

3.

4.

#8 + #3
Shapes

5.

Erase on
dotted
line.

6.

7.

Erase on dotted lines.

↓ NOW YOU TRY ↓

FINAL TSADE DOGGY

1.

2.

3.

4. Don't draw ↖ the dotted lines.

5.

6.

↓ NOW YOU TRY ↓

QOF CRAZY GUY

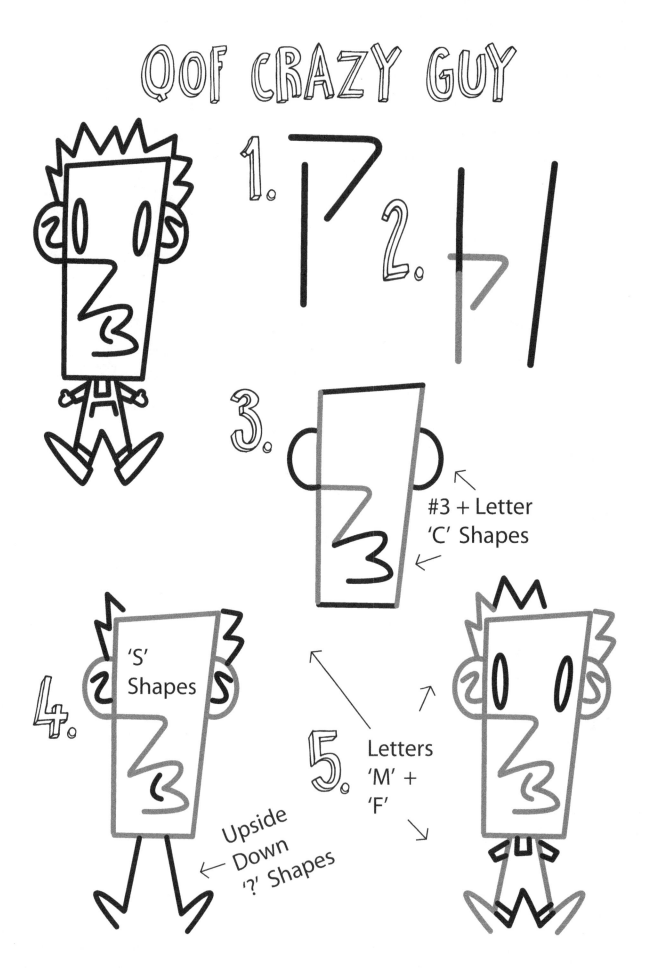

1.

2.

3. #3 + Letter 'C' Shapes

4. 'S' Shapes

5. Letters 'M' + 'F'

Upside Down '?' Shapes

6.

Letter 'M'

#3 Shaped Hands

NOW YOU TRY

RESH CUTESY BEAR

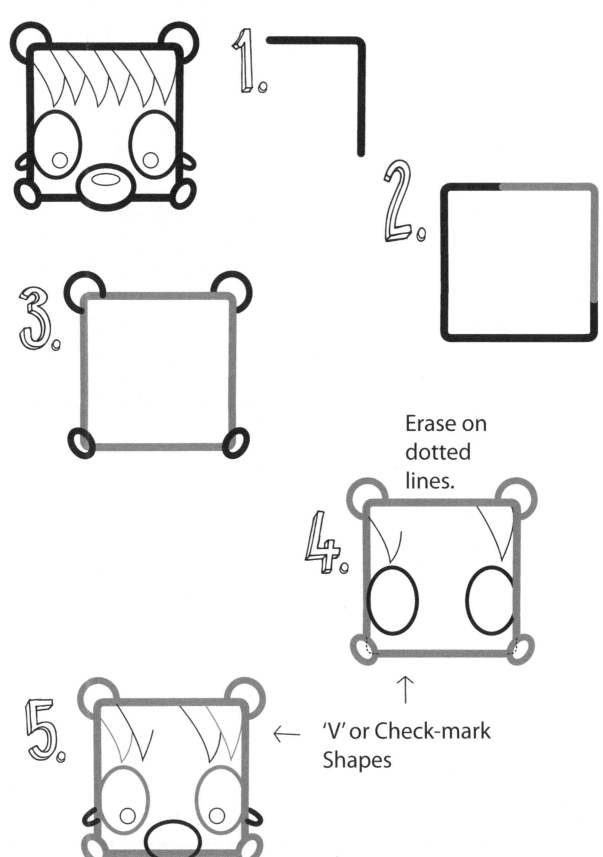

1.

2.

3.

Erase on dotted lines.

4.

↑

← 'V' or Check-mark Shapes

5.

6.

Erase on dotted lines.

⬇ NOW YOU TRY ⬇

SHIN BOY WITH GLASSES

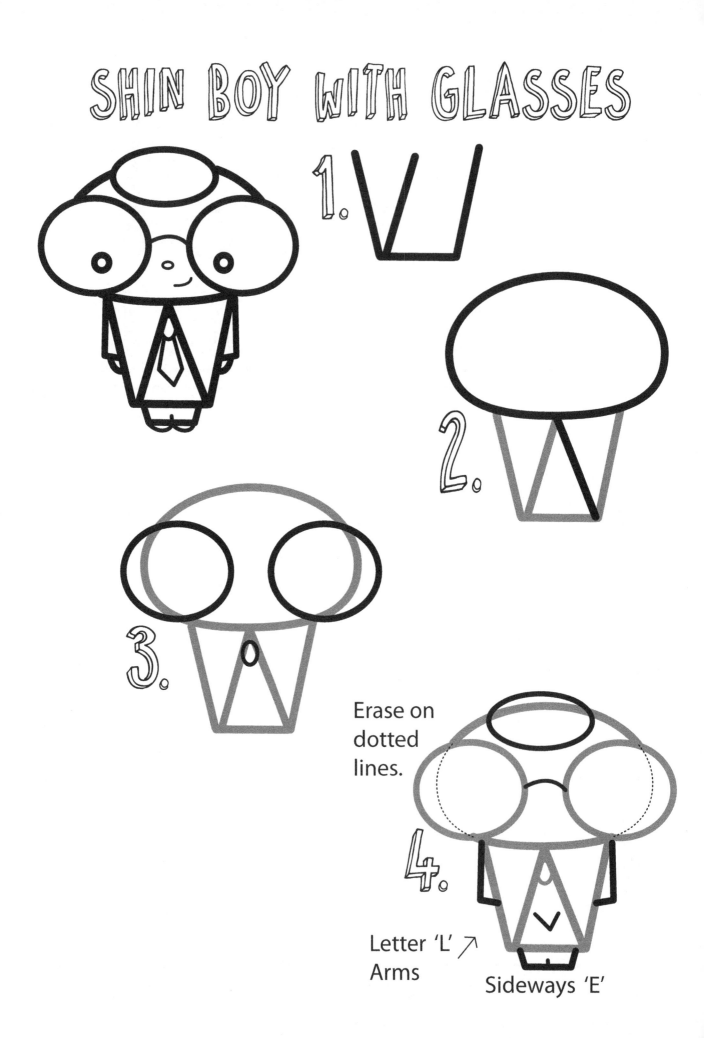

1.

2.

3.

4.

Erase on dotted lines.

Letter 'L' ↗
Arms

Sideways 'E'

5.

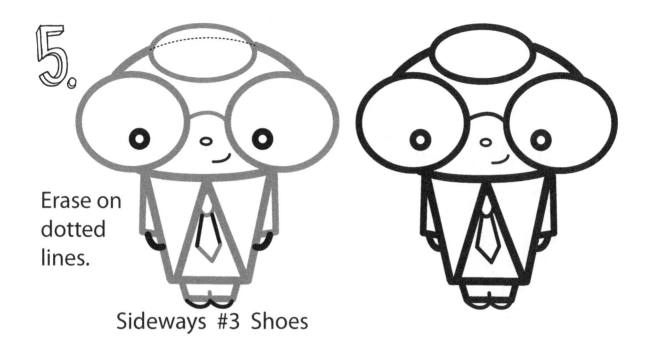

Erase on dotted lines.

Sideways #3 Shoes

↓ NOW YOU TRY ↓

TAV MOODY KNIGHT

1.

2.

3.

4.

#3-Like Shape

Letter 'M'

5.

6.

Letter 'D' + #8 Shapes

7.

↓ NOW YOU TRY ↓

OUR OTHER BOOKS

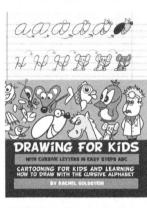

Please Give Us Good Reviews on Amazon! This book is self-published so we need to get the word out! **If You Give us a 5 Star Review**, and Email us About it, We Will Do a Tutorial Per Your Child's Request and Post it On DrawingHowToDraw.com

Made in the USA
Coppell, TX
13 March 2023

14199466R00033